HELPING YOU WORK SMART
NOT HARD ON SOCIAL MEDIA

YOU Smart

365 DAYS OF INFLUENCING

LASHAI BEN SALMI

STEPPING STONES PUBLISHING

YOU Smart

365 DAYS OF INFLUENCING

Stepping Stones PUBLISHING

Published by Stepping Stones Publishing

Copyright © Lashai Ben Salmi

ISBN:978-1-913310-74-5

What is influence?

" The power to have an effect on people or things...

- Cambridge Dictionary

What is a content creator?

> **A content creator is someone who creates appealing and awe-inspiring content for the viewers.**
>
> **The content they create can be educational, or can simply be catchy enough to entertain and grab the attention of any visitor or passerby who wasn't previously interested in your brand. But after looking at the content, they developed a certain interest and visited your webpage or your social media handles.**
>
> **- DigitalMarketing.Org**

YOU Smart

365 DAYS OF INFLUENCING

HOW TO USE THIS BOOK

In this book series you will find 365 daily prompts to inspire you to create.

Everyday open this book to a random page (hopefully you open to a page that isn't the Introduction hahaha), read aloud the content creation prompt/affirmation 3 times, take three deep breaths and then tap into your innate creativity and then begin CREATING!

- Lashai Ben Salmi

INTRODUCTION

HAVE AN IDEA THAT YOU'D LOVE TO SHARE WITH THE WORLD?

The YouSmart- 365 Days Of Influencing system was created to assist you in getting into a daily habit of creating content consistently and with ease.

Content creation can be such an enjoyable process once we understand how to create positive habits and rewards in association to the activity.

Utilising positive prompts around content creating can also maximise the impact that you can have online.

There are more people online NOW more than ever before...

AND they are waiting to hear what you have to say!

In this book you will learn why now is the perfect time to start taking content creation seriously, what I've learned on my journey as a content creator growing my platform to over 50,000 followers and 10,000,000 plus views.

You will also find 365 daily prompts to inspire you to create each and every day.

– *Lashai Ben Salmi*

🔔 **REMINDER**

"I HAVE THE ABILITY TO CREATE AMAZING CONTENT EVERY, SINGLE DAY!"

⬤ CLAIM   ⬤ SNOOZE

WHY SHOULD I CREATE CONTENT?

WHY SHOULD I CREATE CONTENT?

I believe that it is so important to take heed of the fact that the world of predominantly text based content is becoming outdated and video content is in!

Studies have shown that around 80% of all internet activity and traffic will be in the form of videos by 2022 onwards.

Which isn't entirely surprising given that it (video content) accounted for around 65% of internet traffic back in 2016.

Becoming present in online spaces also gives you the ability to engage with the ever growing communities and audiences.

Are you ready to tap into this space?

There are more than 4.55 billion people actively using social media around the world. Of course, there's no guarantee that your content is going to reach all of those people (haha) but I just wanted to bring to your attention the volume of active users on social media platforms.

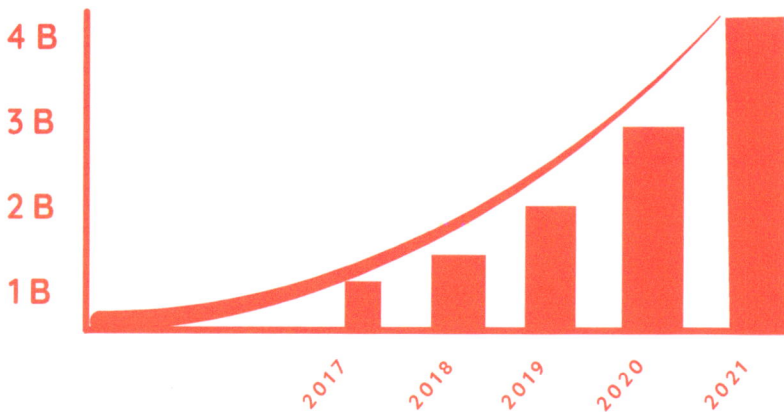

Actively creating content also means that you can amplify your voice, cultivate a community of like minded individuals, increase your reach and impact and also generate opportunities and direct revenue.

WHAT I'VE LEARNT AS A CREATOR

WHAT I'VE LEARNT
AS A CREATOR

As someone who's been a content creator for over a decade I would say that the biggest lesson that I've learned, is that it is so, so important to find what works for you!

I did not create this book to force you to make content every single day, but instead to keep you inspired as a creator every single day.

For some it feels really in alignment to create and post every single day, for others, they like to create and post once a week and some even post once a month.

 It's not about how frequently you post or how much content you make, instead it's about finding and cultivating a creative culture that feels good and is tangible for you to consistently maintain.

WHAT I'VE LEARNT AS A CREATOR

Once you find this, you will see a world of difference in the quality of your content and how it's received when posted.

Another important lesson that i've learnt as a creator is that you don't have to do everything on your own.

Having an accountability or team to support you can be so beneficial.

I developed this book to support the new age creatives, entrepreneurs and businesses in finding unique and

YOU *Smart*

365 DAYS OF INFLUENCING

DAILY CONTENT CREATION PROMPTS, ACTIVITIES & AFFIRMATIONS

You Smart Challenge:

Go LIVE today! Think of 5 things that you could cover and/or who you could go live with.

_____
_____
_____
_____
_____
_____
_____

"When I/we create content,
it feels great!"

"I have the power to create
my own trends..."

Film 1 Video today - it can be between 15 - 60 seconds long.

Your likes don't define
your worth.

Quality over quantity!

Engage with your community
for 30 mins.

It's ok for you to like your own posts, you have to be your biggest supporter at the end of the day, hehehe!

Quality over quantity!

Question for the day:

What is the why behind your platform?

Your following isn't a reflection of your worth!

Share from a vulnerable space today, it could inspire someone!

Question for the day:

"What emotions do I want
my content to evoke?"

What colour are you
feeling today?

Find a group of other like minded creatives.

Create a story.

Tidy up your feeds.

Your feeds don't have to be "perfect" or "aesthetically pleasing" but they should be orderly and congruent.

When someone visits your page or platform they should be able to tell who you are and what you represent!

What is your brand mission?

Today, look for trends in
your niche.

What does your audience want?.. Remember that you dont have to figure this our on your own, create some polls and let them tell you.

What does your
audience need?

"I love being able to positively influence others."

Question for the day:

"How does my current content creation process/ schedule feel?"

Finalise all of your content copy for the week ahead!

You can rest today!

Study your audience, what do they need?

You Smat Challenge:

Speak about you platform/ brand today, whether that's in person (at an event) or online (on a platform like clubhouse).

_____

_____

_____

_____

_____

_____

_____

_____

Network! Network! Network!

Your Network = Your Net Worth

Provide solutions, not just entertainment and commentary!

Spend 1 hour working on your creative skills, be that video editing, photo editing, branding etc.

Create a posting schedule!

Turn to the next page for a template

POSTING SCHEDULE

Monday - Post 1 Picture + 1 Story | 10am

Tuesday - Post 1 Reel + 1 Story | 1pm

Wednesday - Post 1 Video | 4pm

Thursday - Rest Day

Friday - Post A Call To Action | 5pm

Saturday - Post 1 Picture | 10am

Sunday - Post 1 Story | 6pm

POSTING SCHEDULE

Monday -

Tuesday -

Wednesday -

Thursday -

Friday -

Saturday -

Sunday -

Provide solutions, not just entertainment and commentary!

Check in:

Is your current brand identity in alignment with who you are and what you represent?

_____
_____
_____
_____
_____
_____
_____
_____
_____
_____

Show love to another
platform.

it's ok to take a break when you need to, taking time to relax can reignite your creative juices!

Meditate for 15 minutes and clear your mind!

Check out #15ForMeChallenge on Instagram

Question for the day:

Are you enjoying creating content for your platform?

_____

_____

_____

_____

_____

_____

_____

_____

_____

_____

Look into what topics are trending in your niche, it would inspire some new content.

Plan your content a week in advance and put it all in your drafts, trust me it'll make things a look easier :)

Make sure to be active in all content formats!

For example: Reels, Photo Posts, IGTV Video's

You Smat Challenge:

Jump onto social media and share your why!
Share what the mission is behind your platform and
what inspired you to get started!

You can do this in the form of a blog post, a
livestream, a post or even a series of stories.

_____

_____

_____

_____

_____

_____

_____

Ask for help and advice! The only silly questions are the ones that we don't ask!

Upgrade Time

If needed and possible, think about upgrading your equipment / set up.

This could be investing in a ring light, upgrading your phone, getting a new notepad, getting a new camera lense, investing in a whiteboard or even getting a new backdrop.

it doesn't have to be super big or crazy but it is important to invest in things that will make your overall content creation process easier.

Check in:

Is your audience changing?

_____
_____
_____
_____
_____
_____
_____
_____
_____
_____
_____

Look into what topics are trending in your niche, these could inspire you to create some new content.

Check in:

How is your audience reacting to your contnet?

_____

_____

_____

_____

_____

Show the world who
you are.

Spend some time looking into apps and websites that can help you get brand deals and collaboration opportunities.

You Smat Challenge:

Reach out to a brand / platform that you really like and explore the possibility of collaborating with them.

You can start drafting your message below

_____

_____

_____

_____

_____

_____

_____

_____

Network with other creators/ influencers.

Put out a call to action!

Look into outsourcing! You don't have to do everything, do what you enjoy and what you're good at and outsource the rest.

Check in:

How are you feeling today? Keeping yourself happy, well and healthy means that your your brand will feel that way too.

_____

_____

_____

_____

_____

_____

_____

_____

_____

_____

Reach out to a creator, business or platform within your niche and celebrate them!

Repost some content from another platform/ creator that you'd like to support! And remember to tag them.

YO▶U Smart

365 DAYS OF INFLUENCING

USE THE FOLLOWING PAGES TO
CREATE YOUR VERY OWN PRONPTS &
AFFIRMATIONS

YOU*Smart*

365 DAYS OF INFLUENCING

---

365 DAYS OF INFLUENCING

YOU Smart

365 DAYS OF INFLUENCING

DRAW SOMETHING

YOU Smart

365 DAYS OF INFLUENCING

_____

_____

_____

_____

_____

_____

_____

_____

_____

_____

_____

_____

YOU Smart

365 DAYS OF INFLUENCING

DRAW SOMETHING

YOU *Smart*

365 DAYS OF INFLUENCING

_____

_____

_____

_____

_____

_____

_____

_____

_____

_____

_____

YOU Smart

365 DAYS OF INFLUENCING

DRAW SOMETHING

YOU Smart

365 DAYS OF INFLUENCING

_____

_____

_____

_____

_____

_____

_____

_____

_____

_____

_____

_____

YOU Smart

365 DAYS OF INFLUENCING

DRAW SOMETHING

YOU*Smart*

365 DAYS OF INFLUENCING

_____

_____

_____

_____

_____

_____

_____

_____

_____

_____

_____

YOU Smart

365 DAYS OF INFLUENCING

DRAW SOMETHING

YOU *Smart*

365 DAYS OF INFLUENCING

_____

_____

_____

_____

_____

_____

_____

_____

_____

_____

_____

_____

_____

YOU Smart

365 DAYS OF INFLUENCING

DRAW SOMETHING

YOU Smart

365 DAYS OF INFLUENCING

_____

_____

_____

_____

_____

_____

_____

_____

_____

_____

_____

YOU *Smart*

365 DAYS OF INFLUENCING

DRAW SOMETHING

YOU *Smart*

365 DAYS OF INFLUENCING

_____

_____

_____

_____

_____

_____

_____

_____

_____

_____

_____

_____

YOUSmart

365 DAYS OF INFLUENCING

DRAW SOMETHING

YOU Smart

365 DAYS OF INFLUENCING

_____

_____

_____

_____

_____

_____

_____

_____

_____

_____

_____

_____

YOU▶USmart

365 DAYS OF INFLUENCING

DRAW SOMETHING

YOU Smart

365 DAYS OF INFLUENCING

_____

_____

_____

_____

_____

_____

_____

_____

_____

_____

_____

_____

_____

YOU Smart

365 DAYS OF INFLUENCING

DRAW SOMETHING

YOU Smart

365 DAYS OF INFLUENCING

YOU Smart

365 DAYS OF INFLUENCING

DRAW SOMETHING

YOU Smart

365 DAYS OF INFLUENCING

YOU Smart

365 DAYS OF INFLUENCING

DRAW SOMETHING

Lashai Ben Salmi (AKA Shai) is a multi-award winning author, publisher, public speaker, creative director and creator with over 50,000 followers and 10,000,000 plus views.

Her mission is to empower and inspire as many people as possible to turn their dreams into a reality by turning their adversities into empowerment. Lashai is a multiple award winner namely The Korean Cultural Centre UK - Korean Wave Representative Award, PRECIOUS Girls, Rotary and UnLtd to name a few.

She has been a part of the business, entertainment and personal development world since the age of 11. Lashai speaks Korean and works closely with the Korean Cultural Centre and is the co-creator of Hallyu Con. Hallyu Con was awarded and recognised by the Korean Government.

Her signature topics include: Education, Youth Empowerment, Entrepreneurship, Social Media, Travel, Self Belief, K-POP, Entertainment / K-Entertainment, Music, Beauty, Connection, Inspiration and Motivation.

Lashai has been in the entertainment business and personal development world for over a decade. She has spoken from international platforms (Namely, Virgin Money, The Best You Expo, BBC Korea, Yonhap News, KBS, KCCUK, Chelsea FC and StageClip to name a few) to large audiences and is committed to empowering others to follow their dreams. From a young age Lashai has published over 7 books alongside her anti-bullying app.

Lets STAY CONNECTED

WWW.LIFEACCORDINGTOLASHAI.COM

in @LashaiBenSalmi

⊙ @LifeAccordingToLashai

✉ Info@DreamingBigTogether.Com

99 YOUR NETWORK
IS YOUR NET WORTH

www.ingramcontent.com/pod-product-compliance
Lightning Source LLC
Chambersburg PA
CBHW041146210326
41519CB00046B/137